24/3/18
28/10/18

Please renew or return items by the date
shown on your receipt

www.hertfordshire.gov.uk/libraries

Renewals and enquiries: 0300 123 4049

Textphone for hearing or 0300 123 4041
speech impaired users:

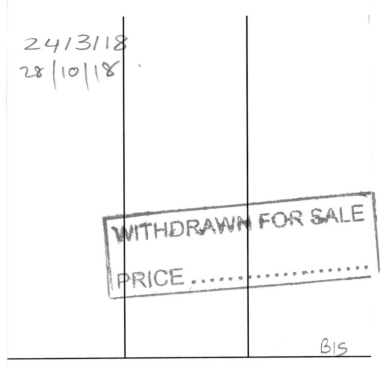

L32 11.16

Hertfordshire

Evolution
Infographics

By Harriet Brundle

Designed by Charlotte Neve

©2017
Book Life
King's Lynn
Norfolk PE30 4LS

ISBN: 978-1-78637-203-1

Written by:
Harriet Brundle

Edited by:
Charlie Ogden

Designed by:
Charlotte Neve

A catalogue record
for this book is
available from
the British Library.

Evolution
Infographics

Contents

Words that are <u>underlined</u> are explained in the glossary on page 31.

Life on Earth

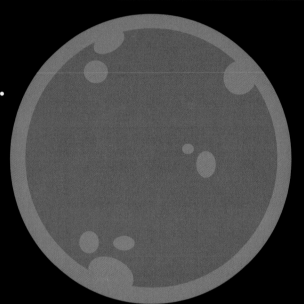

Experts believe that our planet is around 4,543,000,000 years old.

When it first formed, the planet did not have the right conditions to support life. Earth was a ball of red-hot, liquid rock and had an <u>atmosphere</u> made from gases such as carbon dioxide and nitrogen.

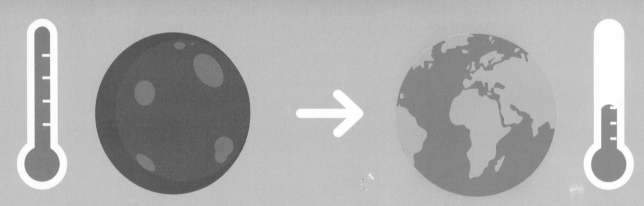

3,800,000,000 years ago, the temperature on Earth began to cool and water appeared on the surface of the planet. It was then that the first life appeared.

Over 70%

of the Earth's surface is now covered in water.

All living things need water to survive. Water also provides a <u>habitat</u> for a vast range of plants, bacteria and animals.

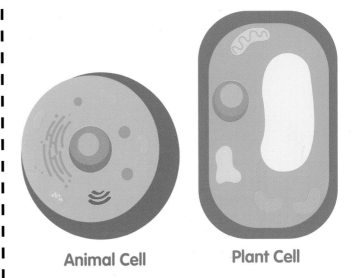

Animal Cell   Plant Cell

All <u>organisms</u> are made of cells. Cells are the <u>microscopic</u> building blocks that make up all life on Earth. The very first organisms on Earth were made of just a single cell.

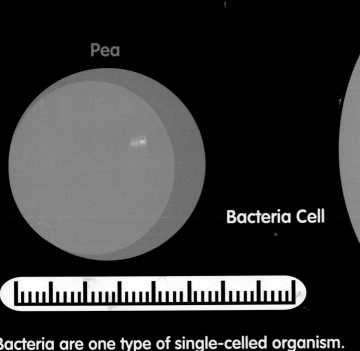

Pea

Bacteria Cell

Bacteria are one type of single-celled organism. It is estimated that bacteria are around 5,000 times smaller than a pea.

9 Million Species!

Every one of the 9,000,000 different <u>species</u> living on Earth began its story with these single-celled organisms.

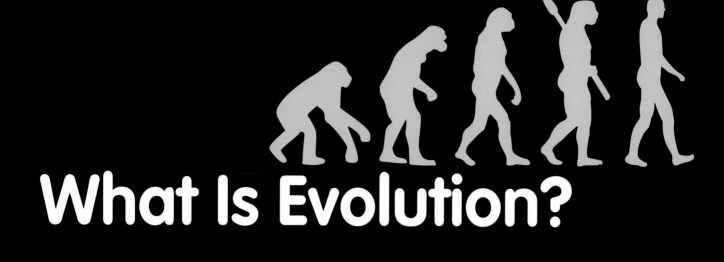

What Is Evolution?

Evolution is a scientific concept that explains how all life on Earth developed over time.

Evolution explains how single-celled organisms <u>multiplied</u> and changed to create all the different species we have on Earth today.

Evolution explains how changes in the <u>characteristics</u> of a species are passed down through the <u>generations</u>.

Evolution is very different to a personal change that an individual might make. For example, if you choose to do lots of exercise to become more muscular, this is not evolution.

Evolution happens very slowly. After the first organisms appeared on Earth, it was between 2,500,000,000 and 3,000,000,000 years before creatures with heads, bodies and tails began to appear.

2,500,000,000
years after the first
single-celled organisms.

3,000,000,000
years after the first
single-celled organisms.

Over 2 Million Cells

Bacteria usually take between 10 and 30 minutes to multiply. This means that within seven hours, one bacterium could multiply to make over 2,000,000 cells!

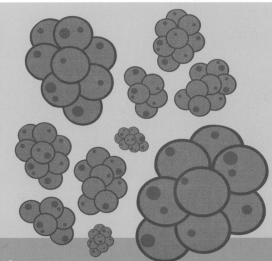

It wasn't until the 19th century that the theory of evolution was developed. A French scientist called Jean-Baptiste Lamarck was one of the first to think about how animal characteristics changed. However, his theory was not entirely accurate.

Growth

Lamarck saw giraffes eating the leaves from the tops of the highest trees. He thought that because giraffes often use their necks to reach food, their necks might grow longer and this characteristic could be passed on to their <u>offspring</u>.

Classifying Animals

All animals are divided into groups based on their characteristics. This is called classification.

Kingdom

We group life on Earth according to its kingdom. There are five main kingdoms: animals, plants, fungi, bacteria and <u>protists</u>.

Phylum

After this, organisms can be grouped based on their shared bodily characteristics. For example, some organisms are vertebrates (meaning they have a backbone) and some are invertebrates (meaning they don't have a backbone).

Vertebrate   **Invertebrate**

Class

Organisms can then be divided into smaller groups called classes. Animals in the same class share even more characteristics. For example, the classes of vertebrate animals are mammals, birds, fish, amphibians and reptiles.

Mammals   **Birds**   **Fish**   **Amphibians**   **Reptiles**

Order

The order that an organism is in usually depends on what kind of food it eats. For example, a mammal that eats meat belongs to the carnivore order.

Carnivores

Family

Species that share lots of similar physical characteristics are said to be in the same family. Big cats, such as lions, tigers and leopards, are all in the same family (called felidae) because they all have long tails and strong jaw muscles.

Genus

Species that share even more characteristics with one another are said to be a part of the same genus. For example, species from the cat family that can roar all belong to the panthera genus.

Species

Living things that share even more distinctive characteristics and are able to <u>reproduce</u> with each other are said to be part of the same species.

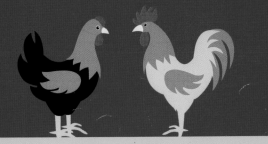

African Elephant

Kingdom:	Animalia
Phylum:	Vertebrate
Class:	Mammalia
Order:	Proboscidae
Family:	Elephantidae
Genus:	Loxodonta
Species:	Loxodonta Africana

Although animals in the same species may have lots of things in common, no two elephants are exactly the same.

One elephant may have a slightly longer trunk, while another elephant may have slightly smaller ears. These differences are known as variations.

Darwin's Theory

In 1831, Charles Darwin decided to go on a journey to learn more about the natural world.

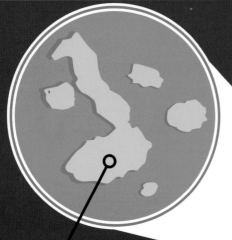

Charles Darwin's journey around the world lasted **5 years.**

Galápagos Islands

During his travels, Darwin visited the Galápagos Islands, which are off the coast of South America.

South America

Darwin found that there were many plants and animals living on the islands that no one had seen before and which could not be found anywhere else on the planet.

One animal that caught Darwin's attention was the Galápagos tortoise.

There are two main types of Galápagos tortoise:

1. The Saddleback Tortoise

2. The Dome-Shaped Tortoise

These tortoises have shells that rise at the front, just like a saddle. This makes it easier for the tortoises to lift their heads high into the air to reach food that grows high up.

These tortoises live on islands with plenty of food close to the ground, meaning that they do not need to raise their heads to eat. Because of this, their shells are rounder in shape and do not rise at the front.

Darwin realised that where the tortoises lived, as well as where their food grew, caused their shells to change shape over time. It was this discovery that began his theory of evolution.

On the Origin of Species

179 years old

One Galápagos tortoise, called Harriet, lived to be 179 years old!

Natural Selection and Survival

Within any species of animal, there will be some variations in their characteristics.

Some variations make an animal's life easier.

This sword-billed hummingbird has an extremely long beak, which can reach all the way into large flowers to get to the <u>nectar</u> within.

Variations can also make an animal's life harder.

Because of their long beaks, some sword-billed hummingbirds find it very difficult to <u>preen</u> themselves. If one hummingbird's beak was too long, it might not be able to preen itself at all, which could cause it to die.

Charles Darwin realised that animals with variations that made their lives easier were more likely to survive. In the same way, animals with variations that made their lives harder were less likely to survive. This is called natural selection.

Some beetles a species are brown and some are green.

Green beetles are more likely to be eaten by birds because they are easier to see. This means that they are more likely to miss out on the chance to produce offspring.

The brown beetles have more chance to produce offspring, meaning that the amount of brown beetles goes up.

Eventually, every member in the beetle species is brown. The species adapted over time to its environment.

1) Owls do their hunting at night, meaning that they need good vision in order to be able to see and catch their <u>prey</u>.

2) The owls that have the best eyesight catch the most prey. Owls with worse eyesight catch less prey and are less likely to survive.

3) The owls that survive are able to reproduce.

4) As a result, owls have developed night vision that allows them to see 100 times better than humans in the dark. This shows how owls have adapted to hunting at night through the process of natural selection.

Inheritance

Animals that survive are able to produce offspring.

When two members of the same species reproduce, the offspring receive a mix of characteristics from the two parents. This is called inheritance.

Offspring

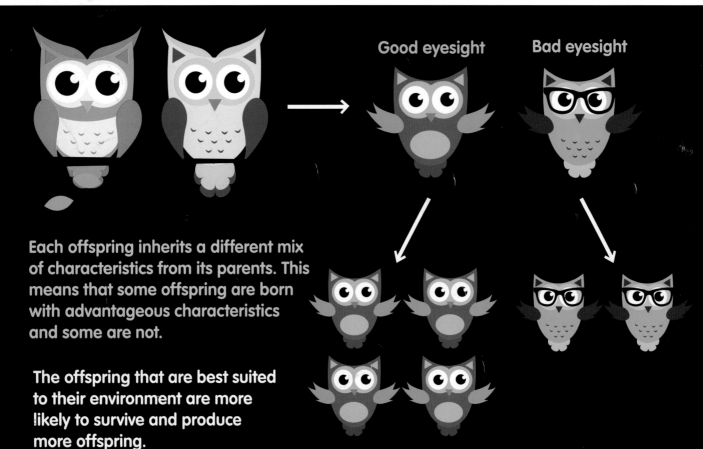

Good eyesight   **Bad eyesight**

Each offspring inherits a different mix of characteristics from its parents. This means that some offspring are born with advantageous characteristics and some are not.

The offspring that are best suited to their environment are more likely to survive and produce more offspring.

Many groups of animals live together in the wild. Within many of these groups, there is a <u>dominant</u> male.

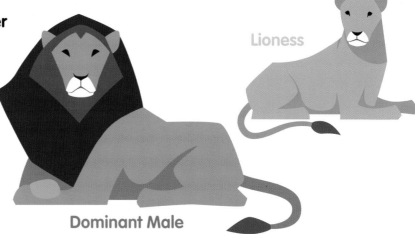

Lioness

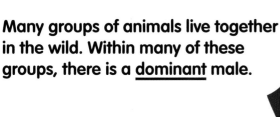

Lion Cubs

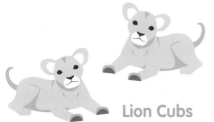

Dominant Male

In gorilla troops, the males fight each other to show who is dominant.

The dominant male is the winner of the fight and is therefore the strongest gorilla in the group.

Dominant Male

The dominant male is the only male that is allowed to mate with the females.

A mixture of his and the females' characteristics are passed to the offspring.

For other animals, the males must impress the females by displaying their best qualities. Male widowbirds jump up and down to attract a mate. The widowbird that can jump the highest and for the longest amount of time will win the female and be allowed to mate with her.

Male widowbird's have tails that are
half a metre long!

Adaptation

Charles Darwin believed that, over a very long period of time, species naturally change and evolve. Evolution helps to make the lives of individuals in a species easier. The long process by which species change is called adaptation.

Adaptation can be broken down into two main categories: behavioural adaptation and physical adaptation.

A species may change the way that it behaves in order to better protect itself from predators or to improve the way that it catches prey.

When a species changes the way that its looks over time, it is called physical adaptation.

An example of physical adaptation is a species that has adapted to have fur on its body to keep itself warm.

Arctic Fox

Many species have adapted to have sharper claws to help them to catch prey.

Polar bears live in the Arctic.

The Arctic

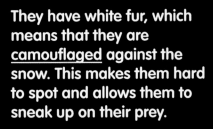

-50 °C

The temperature in the Arctic can reach as low as -50 °C.

Over time, polar bears have adapted to make life in this cold environment easier.

They have white fur, which means that they are <u>camouflaged</u> against the snow. This makes them hard to spot and allows them to sneak up on their prey.

Polar bears can completely close their nostrils, which helps to stop water from going up their noses when they swim.

They have thick fur with a layer of fat underneath. Together, these help to keep the polar bears warm.

Polar bears have wide paws that help them to walk across snow and ice.

Adaptations occur in every species:

Frogs
Adapted to have webbed feet in order to swim faster.

African Elephants
Adapted to have big ears in order to fan themselves in the heat.

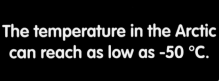

Giraffes
Adapted to have long necks so they can eat leaves that are high up in trees.

Fossils

Fossils are the naturally preserved remains of living things that died over **10,000** years ago.

Scientists use fossils to work out Earth's history and the history of evolution.

When an animal dies, its body may become buried under layers of sand and mud. The fleshy parts of the body rot in the soil, but the harder parts, such as the bones, remain. These eventually become the basis of fossils.

Fossils have been found on every continent on Earth.
There are many different types of fossil.

Body Fossil

The preserved remains of a living thing's body.

Trace Fossil

The preserved remains of things left over by living things; such as footprints, egg shells and nests.

Resin Fossil

The preserved remains of living things, usually plants and insects, that became trapped in tree resin.

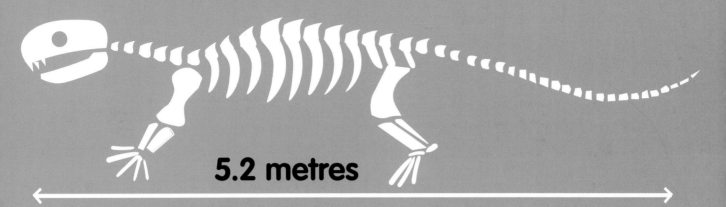

In 1811, Mary Anning discovered the 5.2-metre-long skeleton of a creature that looked like a lizard. This creature, along with others Mary discovered, were part of a group of animals known as dinosaurs.

5.2 metres

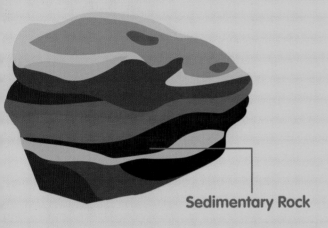

Fossils are usually found in sedimentary rock, which is a type of rock that is formed when layers of <u>sediment</u> are squashed together.

Sedimentary Rock

Fossils can be used to support Darwin's theory, as the <u>fossil record</u> shows how species slowly changed and adapted over time.

Fossils give us clues about the physical and behavioural characteristics of long-dead creatures. For example, a fossil could show that an animal had wings, which would suggest that it could fly.

Fossils can be used to support Darwin's theory, as the fossil record shows how species slowly changed and adapted over time.

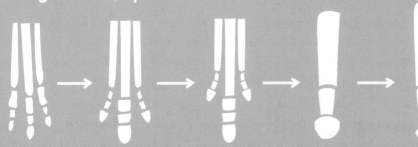

| 60 million years ago | 40 million years ago | 30 million years ago | 10 million years ago | 1 million years ago |

Horse feet adaptation over time.

Human Evolution

The entire process of human evolution has taken around 6,000,000 years. However, modern humans, like us, only appeared on Earth around 200,000 years ago.

The human genus is called Homo and the modern human species is called sapiens. Because of this, we are known as Homo sapiens.

Kingdom:	Animalia
Phylum:	Vertebrate
Class:	Mammalia
Order:	Primate
Family:	Hominidae
Genus:	Homo
Species:	Sapiens

Our <u>ancestors</u> were similar to us, but not exactly the same.

Some of our earliest ancestors lived about 4,000,000 years ago in Africa. Members of this species were more like apes than modern humans, except that they walked on two feet and had human-like hands and teeth.

Early humans began to develop around **2,500,000** years ago.

One of the first human species, which first appeared around 2,000,000 years ago, was given the name Homo erectus. This name means 'upright human' and it was given to Homo erectus because it stood upright. Homo erectus was also the first human species to learn how to use fire.

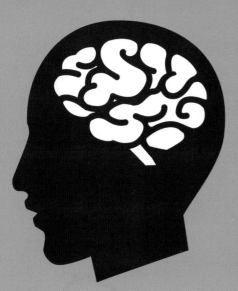

Homo sapiens have very large and complex brains. These have helped us to develop languages to talk to each other and to use tools to build and make things.

It is thought that humans and apes shared a common ancestor that lived in Africa between 5,000,000 and 8,000,000 years ago.

This means that, although we did not evolve from apes, we are distantly related to them.

We would not know this much about human evolution without help from the fossil record.

Early humans lived through one of Earth's ice ages, which ended around 12,000 years ago.

Extreme Evolution

Every species on Earth evolved from the very first life forms that appeared billions of years ago. However, some species have had to evolve in more extreme ways than others in order to survive.

Aye-Aye

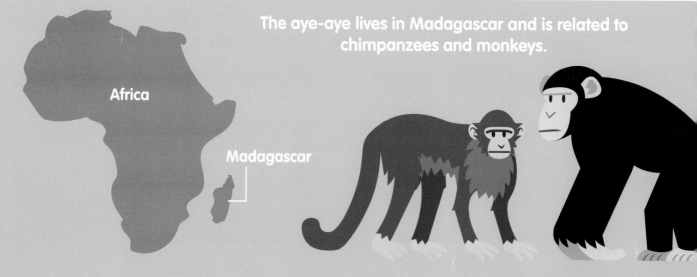

The aye-aye lives in Madagascar and is related to chimpanzees and monkeys.

Africa

Madagascar

Aye-ayes feed on termites and other insects that are found inside wood. Whereas other primates have learnt to use sticks to reach the insects, the aye-aye has evolved to have a middle finger that is incredibly long. This means that aye-ayes can use their finger to reach deep into holes in wood, feel for their food and scoop it into their mouths.

Middle Finger

Termite

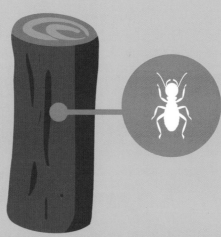

Wood

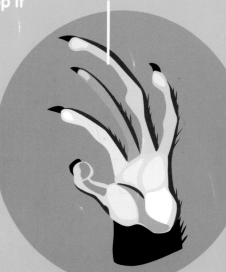

A giraffe's neck can be over 2.4 metres long.

Giraffes are the tallest land animals on Earth and they have an average height of 5 metres.

Giraffes live in Africa and are <u>herbivores</u>.

In order to reach the leaves on the highest branches of trees, giraffes have evolved over time to have extremely long necks and legs.

No two giraffes have the same markings on their fur. This means that giraffes can be identified using their markings in the same way that humans can be identified using their fingerprints.

Green lizards, which previously lived in the lower branches of trees in Florida, were forced out when brown lizards moved into the area.

The brown lizards ate the food in the lower branches of the trees, meaning that the green lizards had to move towards the tops of the trees to find food.

The higher branches were smoother, which the green lizards were not used to. In just 15 years, the green lizards had evolved to have bigger toe pads and stickier scales, which helped them to grip on to the smooth branches higher up in the trees.

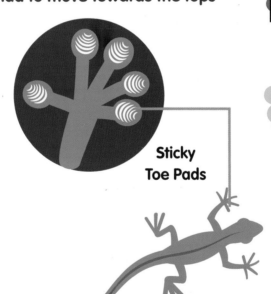

Sticky Toe Pads

Sometimes, a species' physical adaptations do not match its behavioural adaptations. This happens when a species adapts to no longer need a part of its body, but does not adapt to get rid of that part of its body. These features are called vestigial characteristics.

An ostrich has wings but it does not fly. This is an example of a vestigial characteristic. Ostriches have adapted to run around instead of fly. However, ostriches still have the wings that their ancestors used to fly around the skies.

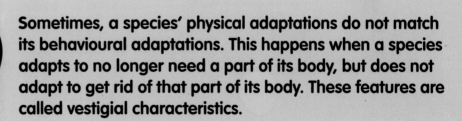

Extinction

A species of animal is said to be extinct when every individual in that species is dead.

When a species becomes extinct, the evolutionary process ends.

Scientists estimate that between **150** and **200** different species of animal, plant and bacteria become extinct every day.

Although extinction is a normal part of natural selection, the rate at which animals are going extinct today is much higher than it used to be. This is because of humans.

Humans hunt lots of species of animal.

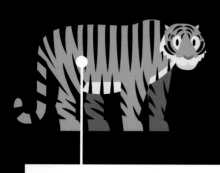

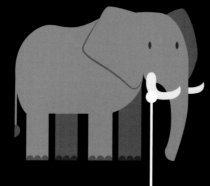

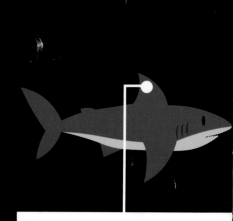

Tigers are hunted for their skins, which are used to make rugs and clothing.

Elephants are hunted for their tusks, which are made of a valuable material called ivory.

Sharks are hunted for their fins, which are used to make shark fin soup.

Earth's climate is always changing. Over the last 4.5 billion years, Earth has experienced both <u>tropical</u> climates and ice ages.

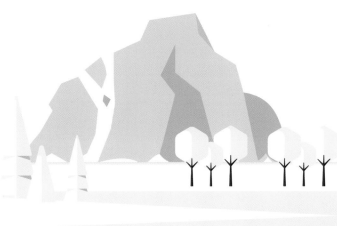

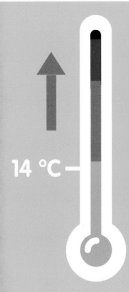

For the last 11,000 years, the Earth's climate has stayed at an average temperature of around 14 °C. However, in recent years, this average temperature has been slowly increasing. This is called global warming.

As the temperature on Earth increases, it causes habitats to change. Animals cannot evolve fast enough to keep up with these changes. This makes it harder for animals to survive and means that more species are in danger of becoming extinct than ever before.

One direct result of Earth's temperature increasing is that ice in the <u>polar regions</u> is melting.

Polar bears hunt for food on top of the ice and, because this ice is quickly melting, there is less space for polar bears to hunt on.

This makes it more difficult for animals in these regions to find and catch food. If this continues, polar bears could become extinct because they cannot find enough food to eat.

Interrupting Evolution

Humans have interrupted the process of natural selection in a number of different ways.

Nowadays, if a person has bad eyesight, they can wear glasses. In the past, humans that had poor eyesight would have struggled to hunt for food and may not have survived long enough to reproduce. Because of this, poor eyesight would not have been passed on to future generations.

6 out of 10

6 out of 10 people now need glasses or contact lenses to improve their eyesight.

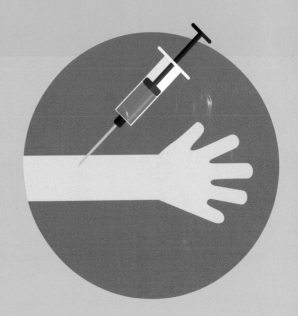

We now have ways to treat infections and diseases that would have killed humans in the past.

By 6 years of age, children can receive as many as 14 different injections to help prevent diseases.

The amount of women who have a narrow <u>pelvis</u> has increased in the last 50 years. In the past, these women and their babies might have died in childbirth. Today, we have medicine that helps mothers and their offspring to survive even if the mother does have a narrow pelvis. Because of this, the disadvantageous characteristic of having a narrow pelvis is being passed on to future generations.

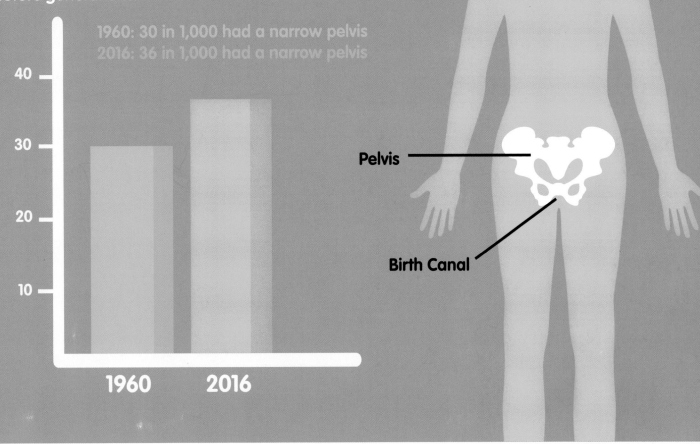

1960: 30 in 1,000 had a narrow pelvis
2016: 36 in 1,000 had a narrow pelvis

Pelvis

Birth Canal

Every ten years, an area of land the size of Britain is made into towns and cities for humans to live in. In the process, many animal habitats are destroyed. Some animals thrive in the new city environment, but many others do not. As humans change environments around the world, we speed up how quickly certain species of animal go extinct.

In Jodhpur, India, humans give lots of food to the local monkeys. There is no competition for food between the monkeys as there is more than enough to go around. Because the monkeys find it very easy to survive in this environment, natural selection can no longer work to adapt and evolve the species.

Evolution Timeline

4.6 billion years ago

Origin of the Earth

530 million years ago

The first fish appeared

225 million years ago

The dinosaurs evolved

3.8 billion years ago

First life appeared

475 million years ago

The first plants on land appeared

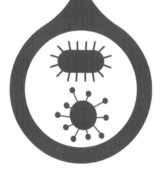

65 million years ago

The dinosaurs became extinct

200 thousand years ago

Modern humans, called Homo sapiens, first appeared

150 million years ago

The first birds evolved

2.5 million years ago

The first human species evolved

Activity

One day, while Charles Darwin was in the Galápagos Islands, he caught a bird. It was a finch. He noticed that its beak was a different shape to the beaks of the other finches he had seen on the island. In total, Darwin found 14 species of finch, each of which had a different shaped beak.

1. Like the tortoises, the finches had adapted to make it easier to eat certain types of food. Can you work out what type of food each finch might have eaten from the shape of its beak?

Large Ground-Finch
broad, strong beak

Warbler-Finch
long, sharp beak

Draw Your Favourite Animal!

2. Think about the habitat it lives in. Think about the different ways it has adapted to its habitat. Has it got sharp teeth? Or lots of fur to keep it warm?

Glossary

ancestors	those from whom one is descended, for example a great-grandparent
atmosphere	the mixture of gases that make up the air and surround the Earth
camouflaged	using its natural characteristics to hide itself in its habitat
characteristics	features of species that help to identify it
dominant	most important or strongest
fossil record	all the fossils that have been discovered and the information derived from them
generations	animals or humans from the same species who are roughly the same age
habitat	the natural environment in which an animal or plant lives
herbivores	animals that only eat plants
microscopic	extremely small in size, only visible using a microscope
multiplied	increased in number or quantity
nectar	a sweet liquid made by plants in order to attract insects
offspring	the children or young of a person or animal
organisms	living things
pelvis	part of the skeleton that is attached to the base of the spine
polar regions	areas on Earth near to the North and South Poles
predators	animals that hunt other animals for food
preen	clean feathers using the beak
prey	animals that are hunted by other animals for food
protists	mould and some algae
sediment	small pieces of material, for example sand, that can form a layer of rock over time
species	a group of very similar animals or plants that are capable of producing young together

Index